PARENTING IS A PARTNERSHIP

The parenthood starts with pregnancy.

Dear Dad, if you're reading this book, it means you have already become a parent. Congratulations! Parenthood is a life-changing experience and one of the most important roles a person can have.

DAD'S ROLE IN MOM'S LIFE
Once you found out that you were expecting a child, everything began to change. Not only did mom's whole body suddenly began to change, but her emotions may have also started to shift. After growing a baby in her body for nearly 9 months, mom's job isn't done after giving birth. The excruciating pains of childbirth are followed by sleepless nights and exhaustion. After delivery, physical and emotional recovery can continue for more than 9 months. But, with your help, it could take a lot less.

You've been mom's support, caretaker, and best friend, constantly showing your unconditional love and appreciation. Dad, everything that you do makes an impact on your family. And that is why, you too, deserve to be recognized and appreciated for all these wonderful things you do to support your partner and your family.

DAD'S ROLE IN CHILD'S LIFE
Dad, as a role model for your kids, your relationship with them has a powerful effect. It influences all of your child's relationships for the rest of their life, including those with friends, lovers, and spouses. Your role doesn't just affect how they will treat others, it also has a bearing on what your child considers acceptable and loving.

"THE MOST IMPORTANT THING IN THE WORLD IS FAMILY AND LOVE."
–JOHN WOODEN

THIS IS MY HANDSOME DADDY

Glue dad's
picture here

ABOUT THE AUTHOR

Ivana Jagodic Meholick is the founder and executive director of a nonprofit public organization, Postpartum Support Center (PPSC) in Northern California. Her work is focused on increasing and improving perinatal mental health awareness, diagnosis, and prevention. To learn more about the PPSC and the work that Ivana does, visit www.postpartumsc.org.

Author: Ivana Jagodic Meholick
Editor: Stefan Meholick
Illustrator: Ameema Sattar
Publisher: Ivana Jagodic Meholick

© 2020 by Ivana Jagodic Meholick

Printed in the United States of America
First Printing, 2020

ISBN: 978-0-578-79872-1

First Edition

ACKNOWLEDGMENTS

Special thanks to my lovely husband, Stefan Meholick and my two sweet daughters, Eva Sofia and Emma Marie, who inspired me to write this book.

THANK YOU, DADDY!

I was very happy to hear from my Mother

How excited you were to become MY FATHER!

Thank you, DADDY, for taking care of Mommy, when I was in her tummy.

And for cooking all those meals; they were so yummy!

Thank you, DADDY, for the back rubs
you gave to Mom

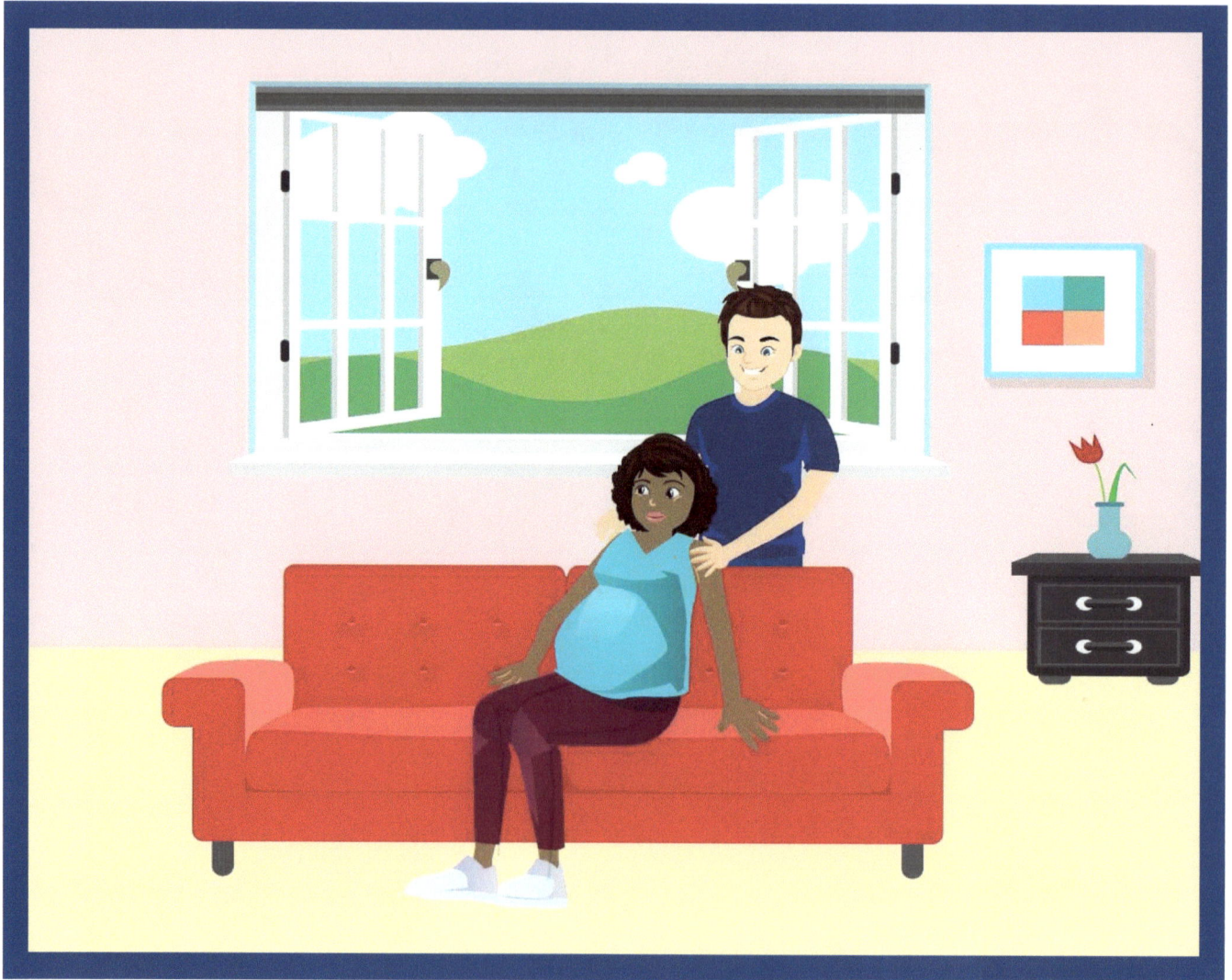

And for going to new-parent classes,
and being so calm.

Thank you, DADDY, for helping Mommy
when she was giving birth

I know it was scary,
but your presence really showed your worth.

I'll never forget, DADDY, the first time I was curled up in your arms

It was then, that I first felt
your incredible charms.

I know, DADDY, that I screamed a lot
and made a mess

Thank you for cleaning up after me and loving
me, nevertheless.

Thank you, DADDY, for changing my diapers and clothes

You care for Mommy, and it really shows.

Thank you, DADDY, for rocking me in your lap

And allowing Mommy to take her much needed nap.

Thank you, DADDY, for playing with the blocks

So Mommy could go out for her evening walks.

Thank you, DADDY, for doing our laundry

Your caring for sure knows no boundary.

Thank you, DADDY,
for giving me a bottle at night

And for allowing Mommy to sleep very tight.

Thank you, DADDY,
for being so patient and loving

I can't wait to wake up
and continue our hugging.

Thank you, DADDY, for being the best FATHER

I could ever wish for!

New Dad of the Year Award

This award goes to

_____

in recognition of his unconditional love, support, patience, involvement, dedication and other caring contributions to the growth of our family.

_____   _____

Mommy   Child(ren)

www.ingramcontent.com/pod-product-compliance
Lightning Source LLC
LaVergne TN
LVHW072112070426
835509LV00003B/134